THE
PRE-RAPHAELITES

THE
PRE-RAPHAELITES

Sandra Forty

BARNES
&NOBLE
BOOKS
NEW YORK

ISBN 0 7607 0750 2 *3138 4570 12/04*

Printed and bound in China

M 10987654321

CONTENTS

THE PRE-RAPHAELITES

First Stirrings

Mid-1850s England was a thriving industrial society, rich on the profits of empire and conquest. Queen Victoria had been on the throne since 1837 and middle and upper class society had settled into comfortable complacency. This was manifested by the art and architecture with which they chose to surround themselves; the extravagance of Georgian taste had quietened down to a sedate pace. In the artistic world the Royal Academy dictated the order of the day. Portrait paintings were pretty but lacking in feeling, as epitomized by Franz Winterhalter, a great favorite with Queen Victoria and the nobility, with his easy, flattering paintings of the royal family and assorted society figures. Another contemporary favorite of the queen's was Sir Edwin Landseer, an unashamed sentimentalist whose dewy-eyed animals found popularity with the general public as well.

Nurtured deep in the bosom of all this propriety, at the Royal Academy Schools, lurked three young men who itched to change the stultifying mores of establishment art. None of them could be described as intellectuals, but they were voracious readers who appreciated stories, legends, and poems of mystery and imagination; romantic tales of heroes and heroines, stirring valor and heart-rending sorrow — qualities they found totally lacking in popular culture. So, with idealistic youthful enthusiasm they decided to do something about it and change the order of the day. The three new friends, Hunt, Millais, and Rossetti discussed and developed their ideas all through the summer of 1848 agreeing on their main direction — that they wanted the vigor and spirit of early Renaissance style brought right up to date with contemporary subjects, but executed in a manner that stayed true to nature. They invited four other carefully chosen friends to join them. In September 1848 at 83 Gower Street, in the heart of the Bloomsbury area of central London and just a short stroll away from the British Museum, the seven friends met.

John Everett Millais, in whose studio they gathered, was only 19; his friend William Holman Hunt was two years older. Of the Rossetti brothers, Dante Gabriel was 20 and William Michael 19 (the only one

not an artist, he worked for the Inland Revenue and was taken on by the group to be its official recorder and secretary). James Collinson was 22 and the prospective brother-in-law of the Rossetti brothers. Thomas Woolner, the only sculptor in the group, was the same age, and Frederick George Stephens was also 20. They chose the name Pre-Raphaelites as a signal that they intended to paint about the subject matter and in the manner of medieval and early Renaissance painters who worked *before* the time of Raphael, whom they considered epitomized the lacklustre, soulless approach to painting that had been executed down the centuries ever since.

In choosing to return to such a mannered style of working, the Pre-Raphaelites were hugely influenced by the writings of John Ruskin, an established and respected art critic and historian, who was himself only in his late twenties. Ruskin had put his ideas on paper in two volumes (at the time, later to total five) entitled *Modern Painters*. The first work was about Turner; more importantly for the Pre-Raphaelites, the second volume was about the sterility of modern art with its lack of attention to detail and neglect of Nature. Ruskin advocated a return to densely symbolic and intensely emotional paintings which in their composition and meaning emphasized the primary role of Nature in all its glory.

The young artists were impressed with his arguments and vowed to bring his ideas right up to date by depicting contemporary subjects in a medieval manner with the use of symbolism to enrich the narrative of the painting. The use of symbolic elements within their paintings was crucial, as this allowed the viewer to discover how the "story" within the painting arose, and how it would develop beyond the confines of the picture. Their subjects were to be of heroes and legendary events — particularly taken from historical and literary subjects. In the early days these were often religious in aspect, although at the time none of them were overtly spiritual.

Furthermore, the Pre-Raphaelites wanted to unite art and literature in a way that had not been explored for centuries — with the notable exception of William Blake. This was particularly at Rossetti's instigation as he had been for years an aspiring poet and lover of literature, and not a particularly good artist.

John Ruskin by John Everett Millais.
In early July 1853 Millais accompanied Mr. and Mrs. John Ruskin
on vacation to Scotland, where they stayed at Brig o' Turk. A
rocky site nearby was chosen for the portrait, the background
featuring the rushing stream to express the transient and
turbulent nature of the elements against the timeless and
unchanging rocks. Progress on the picture was painfully slow; it
took around a year to complete. Millais was paid £350 for it, just
before completion, by Ruskin's father.

The Pre-Raphaelites also took some inspiration from the Nazarene school of German painting, a similar group of young artists, who also had advocated a return to an older, more mannered style of painting, notably following German artists like Dürer.

Talking and close communication with each other was another important element for the Pre-Raphaelite Brotherhood — they bounced ideas off each other and swapped works in an effort to refine and define their new style. For the first attempts to put their ideas into pictures, Millais and Hunt worked together in the former's Bloomsbury studio with the intention of getting their paintings into the Royal Academy (R.A.) Summer Exhibition of 1849. Their efforts crystallized as a modernistic, medieval composition in groupings of flatish, stylized figures, all outlined by harsh naturalistic light which brought out the jewel-bright colors in their rendition of contemporary subjects — all executed with obsessive attention to naturalistic detail. Their perspectives were often distinctly questionable, and the hard outlines to the awkward poses they gave their figures frequently gave the impression of sitting on the canvas rather than belonging to it.

The first real outing for the Pre-Raphaelite Brotherhood came in the R.A. Summer Exhibition, which opened in spring 1849, when three P.R.B. (as each initialled his painting after the signature) works went on view for the first time. These were *Isabella* by Millais, *Rienzi* by Holman Hunt, and *The Girlhood of Mary Virgin* by Rossetti. These three paintings sang out from the rest of the sombre and restrained classical efforts around them. Their vivid colors ravaged the eyes of the critics, who reeled back in horror at the one-dimensional execution of figure and form, and they universally failed to find any meaning in the highly significant usage of symbolism. Their efforts were only quietly received in the press and their enthusiastic attempts at revitalizing the artistic establishment fell on deaf ears and blind eyes.

The paintings were so bright and different because the Pre-Raphaelites had gone to great pains to bring up to date and further develop the old medieval technique of painting color over a white ground. This illuminated the pigment from within, imparting a particularly brilliant and light quality to each painting. This, combined with the minuteness of their brush-strokes and loving execution of even the tiniest and least significant elements in the paintings, gave the pictures an intensity that few artists achieve. As an additional medieval signature, the flattish figures and slightly odd perspectives gave the paintings a very non-contemporary look.

The following year, to follow up and explain some of their thinking about the direction modern painting should take, the Brotherhood collectively produced a small journal entitled *The Germ*. The Rossetti brothers were the prime movers in this endeavor: Dante Gabriel had the ideas and William Michael edited. This was the first magazine ever to be published by an artistic group, a move followed by many polemic artistic movements since. The other Pre-Raphaelites and some of their closer friends contributed; in total they produced four issues, but they were not well received and sold only poorly. The most positive result of *The Germ* was that it became noticed by the art establishment, who were intrigued and amused to learn exactly what the letters P.R.B. stood for.

The spotlight really fell on the Pre-Raphaelites when Millais's untitled picture, variously called *Christ in the Carpenter's Shop* or *Christ in the House of his Parents*, was exhibited at the R.A. in 1850. Already sold to a dealer for around £300, it nevertheless caused a critical outcry and a torrent of abuse. Foremost among the detractors was Charles Dickens, at the time a popular serial author and not yet an important figure in English literature. What caused chief offense was the depiction of the Holy Family as plain, ordinary, poor people who were ugly and dirty with no hint of radiance about them. To add insult to injury, those who chose to do so detected distinct overtones of Roman Catholicism in the offering of blood. The notoriety surrounding the painting grew to such a pitch that a deeply intrigued Queen Victoria asked to see the picture privately, and it was removed from the exhibition for her scrutiny.

The art world as defined by the R.A. was scandalized: a deeply depressed Millais was devastated by the vituperation. However, disappointed but not discouraged, he continued painting in the same style, determined to win through.

Always painfully slow to complete a work, Rossetti finally finished and sent *Ecce Ancilla Domini!* on April 13, not to the R.A. but to the jury-free National Institution. It is a painting about the Annunciation of the Virgin Mary and was planned as part of a triptych. It is predominantly white with only primary colors and gold to relieve the purity. The

ABOVE RIGHT: Teeming crowds out to enjoy themselves as depicted in *The Easter Holidays on Hampstead Heath* published in *The Penny Illustrated Paper* of April 3, 1875.

BELOW RIGHT: The Pre-Raphaelite Brotherhood held many of its meetings in Gower Street, in the Bloomsbury area of central London. Shown here are the open gardens of nearby Bloomsbury Square, which were laid out by the noted landscape gardener, Humphrey Repton.

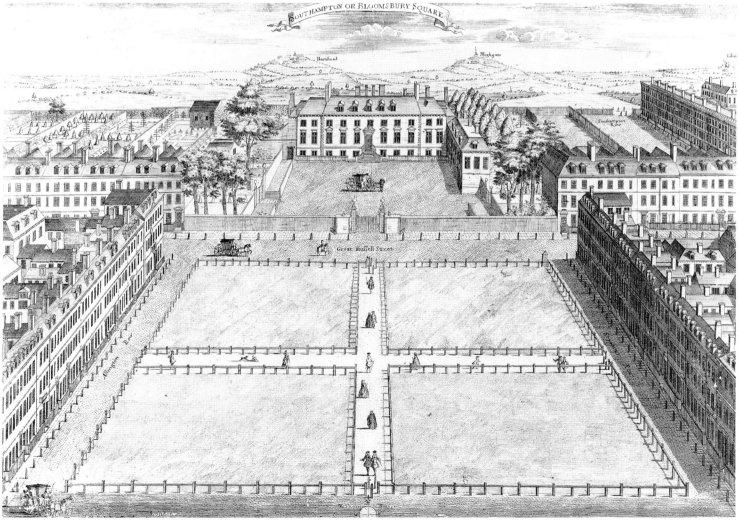

picture was also considered suspiciously Catholic and consequently harshly criticized. It was eventually sold two years later for £50.

This same year another of the founder members, James Collinson, showed the first modern subject at the Academy. *Answering the Emigrant's Letter* dealt with the then important burning issue of emigration. But although he was a member of the Brotherhood, the style of the painting was much more in the traditional Victorian mold. Following the break-up of his engagement to Christina Rossetti, he resigned from the Brotherhood to become once again a Roman Catholic (as he considered the two pursuits incompatible) and study for the priesthood instead. He later abandoned his vocation and returned to painting, although never very successfully.

LEFT: St George's, Bloomsbury (built 1716-30) designed by Nicholas Hawksmoor. At the time the Pre-Raphaelites were working the parish was a very fashionable address, right in the heart of London.

BELOW: William Michael Rossetti was the brother of Dante Gabriel and, although not an artist himself, was one of the seven founder members of the Pre-Raphaelites. It was his job to be the Brotherhood's recorder and secretary.

BELOW RIGHT: Dante Gabriel Rossetti, Algernon Swinburne and George Meredith took No. 16 Cheyne Walk in Chelsea in 1862. In time Rossetti collected around him a menagerie of animals, including many peacocks, which made him a very unpopular neighbor.

Discouraged by the reception their paintings had so far received, the P.R.B. changed direction somewhat from quasi-religious paintings to more acceptable and accessible landscapes. One of the insurmountable problems with their technique and attention to detail was the sheer amount of time each picture took to compose and complete. The attention and care they lavished on every leaf, stone and other normally insignificant detail took long hours of examination and brushwork. Favorite topics were studies of fallen women and the morality problems brought about by illicit relationships. Religious subjects were depicted, not because any of them (other than Collinson) was especially religious, but simply because the Renaissance and medieval painters they admired explored the same subject areas. However, as their religious pictures found no admiration with either critics or, more to the point, art buyers, they rapidly moved away from subjects perceived to be dangerously Popish.

With this change of direction the Pre-Raphaelite Brotherhood itself started to diversify. Rossetti, perhaps because he was initially the least successful of the three pre-eminent artists and also terribly slow to actually complete a work, remained faithful to the original P.R.B. ideals. In fact for the next 10 years he did not exhibit any new works in public, although this had more to do with his inability to complete a painting rather than any public opprobrium. During this time he was unsuccessfully trying his hand at bigger, much more ambitious, canvases. Meanwhile, Hunt and Millais went on together to develop a much more acceptable representational style. Thomas Woolner

eventually made a living out of being an art dealer and Frederick Stephens became known as an art critic, though not in John Ruskin's league. William Rossetti was always the most literary of them all and continued writing; he became the official and most authentic of the Pre-Raphaelite historians as well as his brother's chronicler.

Millais produced three painting for exhibition in 1851, the best known of which is *The Woodman's Daughter*. This depicts the story of a doomed love affair between a humble woodman's daughter and a high-born squire's son; social standing was a very current and contentious theme which the painting addressed directly. The story was inspired by the contemporary poet Coventry Patmore's work entitled *The Tale of Poor Maud*, published in 1849.

Holman Hunt's painting *Valentine Rescuing Sylvia from Proteus* was taken from Shakespeare's *Two Gentlemen of Verona*. By this time savaging the Pre-Raphaelite paintings had become a popular sport entered into with enthusiasm by art critics and anyone else who cared to join in. Holman Hunt despaired of the unequal contest and considered leaving the country altogether. However, Millais, although equally upset, was genuinely worried about his friend and asked Coventry Patmore whether he would petition Ruskin for support. Stirred by the heart-felt appeal John Ruskin, impeccable in his credentials as the premier English art critic of the time, sent the first of two letters to *The Times* on May 13, 1851, supporting the aims of the Pre-Raphaelite Brotherhood and defending its intentions. In particular he praised the power and truth in Hunt's painting. Then, to emphasize the point, he published a pamphlet on Pre-Raphaelitism in which he admitted their failings but insisted that they could only get better and should be treated with more respect. This, coming from such an august personage as Ruskin, forced art skeptics to reappraise the work of the Brotherhood and look at it more seriously.

All this, of course, took time. Though encouraged by Ruskin's brave words, Holman Hunt was still deeply depressed when he went to stay in with Millais at Worcester Park Farm on the south-western outskirts of London. There he began to draft out ideas for the painting which was to become one of the pinnacles of Pre-Raphaelite art: *The Hireling Shepherd*. The subject was taken from the New Testament and marked Holman Hunt's personal conversion to a more religious turn of mind. He became determined to revitalize and modernize religious paintings for the post-Industrial Revolution world. By September 1851 he had dreamed up the companion picture which became *The Light of the World*.

Both paintings are dense with symbolism: in both luxuriant foliage signifies spiritual neglect; the unripe apples in *The Hireling Shepherd* are an allusion to Eve and her fall from grace in the Garden of Eden; there is much more. *The Light of the World* in particular provoked criticism and again Ruskin came to his rescue by writing to *The Times,* explaining its elaborate symbolism. Eventually it would become one of the best-known religious pictures ever; it even went on a national tour of the country so everyone could see it for themselves. However, *The Light of the World* wasn't exhibited until the 1854 Academy Exhibition; meanwhile matters continued as before.

The year 1852 saw the Brotherhood begin to fracture when Thomas Woolner went to seek his fortune in Australia as a gold digger, having realized that he was never going to get anywhere in Britain without commissions for his sculpture. For the other Pre-Raphaelites, things were beginning to improve: their work was not now automatically vilified but was instead taken seriously as a new wave of genuine artistic merit. That same year *The Hireling Shepherd* was shown at the Summer Exhibition, as was Millais's new work *Ophelia* and *A Huguenot*. The latter brought Millais his first real taste of success.

In this same 1852 R.A. exhibition Ford Madox Brown showed *The Pretty Baa-Lambs*, a light, bright, picture much in the Pre-Raphaelite tradition and obviously painted outside in the open air. To complete this impression, it was painted over pure white ground which imparted the vividness of color to the picture. The painting was hung in the Octagon Room in a poor position where the light did not do it justice and those who noticed it reflected disparagingly about it. The painting remained unsold for five years, during which time Brown reworked some of it.

However, by now the Pre-Raphaelite style was gaining adherents among the public as well as with other artists, and their influence was gaining ground. Interestingly, despite their lack of popular and critical acclaim, the Pre-Raphaelites' work had been bought and collected by a few enlightened patrons right from their first appearance. Significantly perhaps, with only one notable exception, their paintings were bought by collectors who were well away from the snobbery of the London artistic circle. One of the first collectors was Thomas Combe, superintendent of the Oxford University Press. He bought principally Hunt and Millais; most of his collection went in time to the Ashmolean Museum in Oxford. Another prominent collector was a Tottenham coach maker, B.G. Windus. Formerly a collector of Turner, he became particularly fond of Rossetti's work and, to a lesser extent, Ruskin. A Liverpool tobacco merchant, John Miller was another admirer of the Pre-Raphaelites and with

A copy of *The Light of the World* by William Holman Hunt. After an initially suspicious reception, this became one of the best-loved and most widely-traveled images of Christ.

his help Liverpool became an early center for their work, primarily by way of exhibitions at the Liverpool Academy.

Painters such as Arthur Hughes and Robert Martineau took up the Pre-Raphaelite cause, espousing Nature and truth in the rendition of modern subjects. Martineau had also been a pupil of Holman Hunt; the painting for which he is best known, *Last Day in the Old Home,* is typically Pre-Raphaelite in its choice of a contemporary topic illustrated with almost photographic precision. Arthur Hughes, a more prolific artist, was also more obviously Pre-Raphaelite with his choice of romantic subjects, typically of lovers and rustic scenes. He was never a member of the Brotherhood, although he too had been a pupil at the R.A. Schools and was a friend of Millais, Hunt, and Rossetti.

The Brotherhood reached a far wider audience when they had some of their paintings exhibited as part of the British section of the Paris Exhibition of 1855, where they received favorable critical attention. In 1857 Pre-Raphaelite pictures were shown in the Manchester Art Treasures Exhibition, and in the same year some of their works were sent to the United States to take part in an exhibition there.

By this time the members of the Brotherhood had each gone in their own direction. Only Rossetti stuck to the original ideals, although he lacked the technical ability to paint with the precision required in the original manifesto. Never easy with oil paints, he started using watercolors and consequently painting on a much smaller scale. Over time he developed a highly individual technique which suited his limited abilities and, more importantly, a few keen patrons. Millais still adhered to the Pre-Raphaelite pin-point detailing but he found he achieved most popular success with scenes depicting sentimental stories about lovers. By the 1860s he had left Pre-Raphaelitism behind and had abandoned the style altogether.

With the success of *The Light of the World* Holman Hunt found himself drawn to religious subjects and in time he became best known as an out-and-out religious painter. In all he made four visits to the Holy Land; on the first journey, which lasted 1854–56, he returned with the weirdly composed and colored painting entitled *The Scapegoat.* It was the culmination of his quest for authentic biblical locations and was set along the arid shores of the Dead Sea. True to the precepts of Pre-Raphaelitism, it was intensely symbolic — in essence, of Christ taking onto himself the sins of the world. Hunt continued painting in the Pre-Raphaelite tradition, rendering his subjects with precision, all the while interwoven with elaborate symbolism.

The Second Coming

The second great arising of the Pre-Raphaelite movement again had Dante Gabriel Rossetti instrumental from the beginning. Life had proved hard for him, his romantic spirit too often distracting him away from sensible means of making a living. However, he had his admirers and with their help succeeded in tendering for an important — and big — commission to paint murals in the Oxford Union building. Needing help for this huge undertaking, he looked around among the students for suitable helpers. Maybe by coincidence, and counting himself, seven members were again collected to form a group that also became known as Pre-Raphaelites. Two undergraduates immediately stood out — William Morris and Edward Burne-Jones — and Rossetti had little trouble in recruiting them. The other four were Arthur Hughes, Val Prinsep, John Hungerford Pollen, and Spencer-Stanhope.

William Morris and Edward Burne-Jones were both undergraduates at Exeter College, Oxford, and heading for safe careers in the church. They had already become good friends who enjoyed each other's company and shared an admiration for poets such as Tennyson, Keats, and Shelly as well as the whole world of medieval romance, especially as described by Mallory. They visited churches together, looking at the illuminated manuscripts and taking rubbings from the memorial brasses. Together with friends of a similar persuasion, they called themselves the Brotherhood. Initially unaware of the Pre-Raphaelites and their paintings, once they became familiar with their works they determined to change the course of their lives and devote themselves to art and design. To achieve this end, Morris decided to become an architect, and secured a job at the Oxford offices of G.E. Street known for their Gothic revival buildings. Burne-Jones decided to be a painter and determined to meet Dante Gabriel Rossetti whose

ABOVE RIGHT: Just north of High Holborn lies Red Lion Square. were Dante Gabriel Rossetti lived at No. 17 for a year in 1851. William Morris and Edward Burne-Jones shared the same address between 1856 and 1859. The landlord insisted "that the models are kept under some gentlemanly restraint as some artists sacrifice the dignity of art to the baseness of passion."

BELOW RIGHT: A view from the top of Hampstead Heath looking towards the center of London. Ford Madox Brown painted extensively in the Heath area during the 1850s before moving down the hill a short distance to paint *Work* in Heath Street, Hampstead.

Dante Drawing the Head of Beatrice galvanized him to artistic endeavors.

Burne-Jones at last got to meet Rossetti at his studio near Blackfriars. They took to each other and Burne-Jones began painting under his guidance. Morris remained training as an architect back in Oxford but visited London once a week to see his friends. However, as luck would have it, his firm soon removed to London, and Morris and Burne-Jones took rooms together in Red Lion Square. Under the double — and no doubt unrelenting — influence of Burne-Jones and Rossetti, Morris decided to abandon his apprenticeship and devote himself to painting. The rooms they shared just off Holborn were unfurnished, and the pair took to making and decorating their own furniture. Morris in particular found this a revelation, and discovered in himself a predilection and a delight in creating pattern as well as a remarkable ability to design it.

At around the same time Rossetti, after petitioning heavily for the job, finally landed the commission to decorate the Oxford Union Building. He immediately summoned Burne-Jones and Morris from London, John Pollen who had already painted the ceiling of Merton College Chapel, and artistic friends Spencer Stanhope, Val Princep and Arthur Hughes. Together they painted and laughed as work progressed through that summer. Everything revolved around Rossetti, whose strong personality drove and invigorated the work. The job was to paint 10 bays around and above the gallery encircling the Union debating hall. The subject chosen were scenes taken from Mallory's *Morte d'Arthur*. The new walls still had damp plaster when they commenced fresco work, which unfortunately, and rather disastrously, none of them knew how to apply correctly. The project was never completed, which hardly mattered, as the paint sank in or flaked off the walls and within six months much of the work had disappeared.

By autumn the group had more or less dispersed and only the three principals were left in Oxford. Then, one evening Rossetti and Burne-Jones met and became acquainted with the 18-year old Jane Burden, whom Rossetti persuaded to sit for him. From then on she became the prototype Pre-Raphaelite woman — clouds of long, dark, wavy hair, long nose, full mouth and large eyes below heavy brows. William Morris instantly loved her and made her the subject of one of his very few paintings, *Queen Guinevere* (1858).

William and Jane married and for their marital home in Bexley Heath Morris decided to commission an architect friend from his old firm, and then design and build all the furniture and furnishings himself. Thus the idea for the firm of Morris, Marshall,

Faulkner & Co. emerged. This was to be a collection of designers and craftsmen who would return to medieval values of quality and design but with modern furnishings. Rossetti was one of the founder members of the firm, although he was personally more interested in pursuing his watercolor work and never took much part in its proceedings.

So the influence of the Pre-Raphaelites was dispersed on the winds, the originality and creativity of the movement was over, but the momentum they started carried their images and ideas out into the greater world beyond the closed doors of the art establishment.

Influence

The Pre-Raphaelites were part of a general artistic swell which arose all around western Europe at much the same time. They were the offspring of an earlier idealistic spirituality which had its progenitor in the wildly ecstatic work of William Blake. Rossetti's later work, particularly with intense watercolors, conveyed an other-worldliness that European painters found inspiring and intriguing; and his studies of exotically clad women were also influential abroad. By the time the Pre-Raphaelites had burnt out, the malign influence of the Royal Academy had been broken, and it was never to regain its pre-eminence, although it has remained an important bastion of British art. The Brotherhood was instrumental in this change, and can take much of the credit, but times were inexorably changing and a new vision was about to sweep the established art world aside. The final nail in the coffin of the Royal Academy was the opening of a rival exhibition venue, the Grosvenor Gallery, in 1877. It not only showed contemporary young British artists but also the newly influential French artists of the day.

Burne-Jones personally provided huge stimulation for the early developers of the Symbolist Movement which arose in and around Paris and he was one of the major creators of fin de siècle art. One of his biggest admirers was Aubrey Beardsley, whom he advised and encouraged to become an artist. Beardsley took Burne-Jones's lyrical, linear approach and developed it further for his graphic black and white pictures. Beardsley was one of the earliest

RIGHT: James Abbot McNeil Whistler was in the Pre-Raphaelite circle in the 1860s. He was for a time influenced by the medieval-like attitudes and drapery of Rossetti's figures in particular, as here, in *The Little White Girl; Symphony in White No 2.*

RIGHT: Aubrey Beardsley as a young man idolized Edward Burne-Jones and took his advice to become an artist. His early work reflects the Pre-Raphaelite influences very clearly, especially the linear work of Burne-Jones and William Morris. Here *The Dancer's Reward*, 1894, an illustration executed for Oscar Wilde's *Salome*.

CENTRE RIGHT, TOP: This small sketch by Aubrey Beardsley, *Hamlet Patris Manem Sequitar* (1891), clearly shows the influence of Burne-Jones in the elongated figure and tight perpendicular ground.

CENTRE RIGHT, BOTTOM: In 1892 Aubrey Beardsley was commissioned to illustrate a new edition of the *Morte d'Arthur* by the publisher, John Dent. His work is a key link between the later Pre-Raphaelites and the European Symbolists.

FAR RIGHT: The Arts and Crafts Movement gave the opportunity to many young artists to get their work noticed. This is an illustration from *The Studio* by Will Bradley.

founders of Art Nouveau style and certainly one of the most distinctive.

The linear quality of the work, particularly of the later Pre-Raphaelites Edward Burne-Jones and William Morris, had echoes in later Victorian artists whose main métier was book illustration, great linear artists such as Arthur Rackham and Cayley Robinson and then decorative giants like Walter Crane, as well as many lesser-known imitators and followers.

Working at much the same time as the Pre-Raphaelites, but more within the aegis and patronage of the R.A., were fine painters such as Lord Leighton, Albert Moore, Frederick Watts, and the Dutchman, Alma-Tadema. Although they were loathe to admit it, their work owed a lot to the later Pre-Raphaelites, and Burne-Jones in particular, whose romantic style had opened the eyes of the public to the opportunities open to artists whose imagination and artistic vision could roam beyond the present to a mystical past. Such classical artists, however, were emphatically not Pre-Raphaelites — a point about which Lord Leighton in particular was adamant. Where the Pre-Raphaelites looked back to medieval times as being the epitome of artistic achievement, the Classicists — like Leighton and Alma-Tadema — harked back much further to ancient Greece, Rome, and Egypt for their inspiration. They claimed that the basis of their work was factual, whereas the Pre-Raphaelites were merely fanciful: artistically they shared little common

ground other than their attention to detail and the "finish" of the painting, which in the case of the Classicists was almost photographic in its quality.

For much of the twentieth century the paintings of the Pre-Raphaelites has gone unappreciated by both art historians and the general public alike. Their work was submerged by the great uprush of the Impressionists and then modernists of all persuasions. For years their personal voyage away from establishment artistic values was put down to a youthful over-enthusiasm for myth and legend, and an over-impressionable voracity for the works and thoughts of John Ruskin. A reappraisal of the work of the Pre-Raphaelites came about in the 1970s when an interest in Art Nouveau style generally led people back to the roots of their influence — a time when romanticism and imagination was appreciated. Their work was re-examined more closely and with a greater appreciation for their abilities and influence on artists to follow. Now a number of the members of the Pre-Raphaelites are considered to be among some of the very best artists that Britain has produced and their work is highly sought after on the extremely rare occasions it comes on the open market.

Outline Biographies

EDWARD BURNE-JONES
1833–1898

Burne-Jones is the most important and the best painter of the second wave of Pre-Raphaelites. A poetic young man from Birmingham who, like Morris, was preparing for a career in the church, he never had any academic art training and consequently developed his own very distinctive approach, using medieval models as his template but invigorating them with a completely fresh and modern look.

Burne-Jones used as his subjects a wide range of legends, myths, and spiritual stories — using images and ideas gathered not just from the Christian viewpoint as previous artists had done. He was not much appreciated early on in his career; it took the opening of the Grosvenor Gallery in 1877 — for anti-R.A. artists to show their work — before he received much critical notice.

Edward Burne-Jones traveled to Italy in 1859 with John Ruskin where he saw and greatly admired the early Italian Renaissance painters like Botticelli, da Vinci, Michaelangelo, and Mantegna from whose work he took a great deal of inspiration. He greatly admired Dante Gabriel Rossetti and was deeply in his thrall until around the early 1860s when he developed his own distinctive style.

Characteristic of the Pre-Raphaelites, Burne-Jones took a very long time to compose and paint his pictures; he would frequently leave them for a time and go to work on other paintings, thus working on two or three concurrently.

Burne-Jones was one of the first artists to break away from the conventional canvas size and presentation of paintings. He was fascinated with strongly linear composition which suited his somewhat flat technique (especially with draperies) and the challenges of presenting and exaggerating the subjects with the size and shapes of his canvases. Sometimes this meant using long and horizontal fields; other times, and more often, extremely tall and narrow as in *King Cophetua and the Beggar Maid* and *The Golden Stairs*. This highly mannered style of dreamy, literary romance exaggerates and encapsulates the subject and gives it an other-world intensity that would be lost on a bigger canvas. This also altered the perception of perspective: either particularly deep or very compressed. His figures are always graceful and often possess a languid quality much copied by later Victorian artists such as Lord Leighton and Alma - Tadema. Color was not so important to him as form; indeed his coloring is often sombre and drawn from a very narrow palette.

Furthermore his figures often possess an androgynous quality — many of the heroes of his pictures have distinctly feminine looks.

By around 1885 his work began to achieve high prices at auction and he became collected. His reputation continued to grow very slowly but inexorably, until he eventually became the hero of the Aesthetic Movement of the 1880s. Burne-Jones was invited to exhibit at the Paris Universal Exhibition of 1889 where his work was a great triumph with the public. Consequently he was awarded a first-class medal, something that really established him as an important artist and made him famous in Europe. Fame at home was reinforced by the exhibition of his *Briar Rose* series — based on the story of Sleeping Beauty — at Agnew's gallery in London in 1890.

Burne-Jones did other design work for Morris and Co. for whom he produced art glass window designs and tapestries. He had a special love of the medium and became an expert craftsman to such an extent that he lectured on the subject at the Working Men's College. As with the tapestries, figures were his speciality. He was made a baronet in 1894.

Edward Burne-Jones was the first Pre-Raphaelite to be truly appreciated beyond British shores and has been credited with being one of the major progenitors of *fin de siècle* art in Europe.

WILLIAM SHAKESPEARE BURTON
1826–1916

Born in London, the son of actor and dramatist William Evans Burton, he studied art at the Government School of Design, then at Somerset House and finally at the R.A. Schools. Burton had intermittent success as a painter; the height of his achievement was *The Wounded Cavalier*, which was well received by art critics and the public. This was his only work in the Pre-Raphaelite manner, with absolutely minute detail in the closely observed plants and flowers. The following year the R.A. rejected his submission and, deeply discouraged, his health failed him. From 1868 to 1876 he lived in Italy. In 1882 he suffered a complete breakdown and stopped painting altogether until about 1889, by which time he was generally forgotten. Critical opinion of his painting improved in the 1890s when he started to enjoy a degree of success. He went on to become an early Symbolist with his painting *The World's Gratitude*. He died in Lewisham on January 26, 1916.

CHARLES ALLSTON COLLINS
1828–1873

Born in Hampstead, his father was the genre painter William Collins, and his older brother the novelist Wilkie Collins. The latter was a friend of Millais and introduced the pair in 1850 when they were both at the R.A. Schools. Millais and Collins spent the next summer painting together in Oxford, Millais on *The Woodman's Daughter* and Collins on *Convent Thoughts,* in the garden of the Clarendon Press. This painting reflected his somewhat aesthetic, introspective sensibilities.

When Collinson withdrew from the Brotherhood, Millais wanted Collins to join in his place, but Deverell was chosen ahead of him by the other P.R.B. members. Millais refused to agree to Deverell's membership. The factions split — Millais, Hunt, Rossetti, and Stephens wanted Collins — Woolner emphatically did not, and William Michael Rossetti sympathised with Woolner's view that Collins had not established himself as having any legitimate claim to be considered a member. Furthermore, he feared that the good relations between the Brotherhood members would be jeopardized by Collins's inclusion. In the event, nobody was allowed to replace Collinson. For a period, Collins fell in love with the rather serious-minded Maria Rossetti, but she wasn't interested in him. In the late 1850s he gave up painting for writing and in 1860 he married Kate, the daughter of Charles Dickens, for whom he subsequently did some illustration work. He died after a long illness in April, 1873.

WILLIAM DYCE
1806–1864.

A Scotsman from Aberdeen, Dyce was a formative influence on the early thinking and development of the Pre-Raphaelites. They noticed in particular the intense, even photographic, quality he brought to his landscapes. He in return was influenced by the Pre-Raphaelites, though he was not invited to become a member. He produced his most memorable work *Pegwell Bay, Kent* in 1858.

WILLIAM POWELL FRITH
1819–1909

Frith's father, a Harrogate innkeeper, was very keen for his son to become a great artist. Initially he worked as a traveling portrait painter, but after 1850 specialized in historical scenes and genre subjects. Frith became in time one of the most successful painters of contemporary life. His best known paintings are *Ramsgate Sands*, (1853), *Derby Day* (1858) and *The Railway Station* (1862). These were all painted in minute detail but on large canvases, and included an enormous number of well-known figures and a huge amount of anecdotal incident. Frith's work was so popular with the general public, who arrived in enthusiastic numbers, that barriers had to be erected at the R.A. to protect the paintings from the crush. Frith traveled a good deal in Holland and visited Italy; he published three volumes of reminiscences of his life and journeying.

WILLIAM HOLMAN HUNT
1827–1910.

In character Holman Hunt was completely different to Millais. Where Millais was affable and generous Holman Hunt was arrogant and unlikeable. His father was a warehouse manager in Cheapside, London, who ran an evangelical home where the young Holman Hunt spent considerable time reading the Bible. Holman Hunt left school early and went to work as a clerk at the age of 12. But office work bored him, he dreamed instead of being an artist, although he lacked the natural talent to be one. What he did have in abundance, however, were imagination and vision — rare qualities at a time when society was thrusting forward with post-Industrial Revolution fervor.

Eventually he persuaded his reluctant parents to allow him to attend the R.A. Schools where he could pursue his ambition to be a painter. There he was soon completely disillusioned by contemporary British art, in which he could find nothing to emulate or admire. However he read John Ruskin's second volume of *Modern Painters* and was hugely impressed by his argument that artists should return to the style of late medieval and early Renaissance painters,

This smaller painting by William Holman Hunt of *The Scapegoat* was done in tandem with his larger version and used to formulate and develop his ideas and presentation of the subject. Amongst other changes in the larger version, the color of the goat is changed to white and the rainbow omitted.

particularly Venetian, in their style of art. This appealed to the young Holman Hunt, who had spiritual leanings, especially the idea of bringing symbolic realism into modern art, so that the viewer could read with the help of metaphors more than the story apparently tells.

He met and became good, if unlikely, friends with Millais, another art student at the R.A. Both of them fostered the desire to get a painting into the 1848 R.A. Exhibition. Hunt in particular was anxious to get an acclaimed painting exhibited as he badly needed to sell paintings to make a living. They discussed ideas and techniques and painted in the studio together on their offerings for the exhibition. But while Hunt's painting was accepted, Millais's was not. Hunt had chosen a subject from a little known poem by a fairly obscure poet who had died in 1821: the poem was *The Eve of St Agnes* and the poet Keats. But a recently published biography and the re-publication of Keats's works led to a reassessment of his intensely visual poems. Furthermore, he too, had been very interested in Italian art before Raphael's time.

Holman Hunt chose a scene from the poem when the hero Rienzi decides to revenge the death of his younger brother. The painting was painted in a flat medieval style and called *Rienzi*; it included a number of symbolic emblems, including a circlet of flowers around the sword hilt. Rossetti posed for Rienzi and Millais for his dead brother. Much of the landscape was painted outside on Hampstead Heath but the figures were all done indoors. The painting bore the mysterious appellation P.R.B. The work was generally well received and considered to show great promise.

By 1850 Hunt had finished *A Converted British Family Sheltering a Christian Missionary from the Persecution of the Druids* — better known simply as *The Missionary*. This picture appeared in the same exhibition as Millais's *Christ in the House of his Parents*. Both paintings received harsh criticism, although the main thrust was aimed at the latter. *The Missionary* was initially Hunt's entry piece for the Royal Academy Gold Medal Contest but the painting's most important consequence was that, through the good offices of Millais, Holman Hunt got to meet Mr. and Mrs. Thomas Combe. He was in his fifties and Superintendent of the Oxford University Press. He and his wife became very fond of Holman Hunt and in the course of time took on the role of surrogate parents to him as well as important patrons of the Pre-Raphaelites generally. Help also came in the shape of John Ruskin — the very man whose literary criticizm had opened Holman Hunt's eyes in the first place to symbolism and early Italian paintings. Ruskin wrote his influential letters to *The Times* and got to meet the artists themselves. In time he too became great

A sketch of William Holman Hunt by Millais.

friends with Holman Hunt and did a considerable amount to bolster the often discouraged and despairing Hunt.

When Holman Hunt accompanied Millais to Worcester Park Farm he was in a very demoralized and depressed state of mind. But he started to conceive a picture that was apparently taken from *King Lear* but was in actual fact inspired by the New Testament, specifically Chapter 10 of St John's Gospel. The painting was finally entitled *The Hireling Shepherd* and became in time one of the best known of all Pre-Raphaelite works.

Around the same time he decided to paint a companion piece to symbolize and record his conversion to religion: it proved a turning point in his artistic and spiritual life. The picture was *The Light of the World* begun in 1851. This symbolized Christian salvation coming to a sinful world through the overabundant and sadly neglected undergrowth. To achieve realism he did much of this painting at night by the light of a lamp. The two works are full of symbolic meaning, the light and dark, the luxuriant, uncontrolled plants, and so on. He developed his own artistic language to describe the style that he termed "symbolic realism." With this he wanted to bring religious painting, specifically Christian, up to date for a post-Industrial audience to understand and appreciate, and to give modern churchgoers their own contemporary iconography.

When the painting went on exhibition in 1853 it was harshly criticized initially as having suspiciously Catholic leanings, and once again Ruskin came to his rescue via *The Times* with a letter explaining its symbolism. Curiosity about the painting reached such a pitch that it went on a national tour. *The Light of the World* became so popular that Hunt was asked to paint a larger copy, which he did with an assistant's help (1900–04;, this then toured the colonies until it finally came back to England, when it was presented to St. Paul's Cathedral in London.

For the 1852 summer exhibition Holman Hunt painted the secular version of his religious work, *The Awakening Conscience*. In this picture a young woman starts up from the lap of her lover, struck by the sudden knowledge of her sin. The entire painting can be read for symbolism: the cat tormenting a bird, the scattered music sheets on the floor, the tangled embroidery threads, and so on.

As a natural extension of his ever increasing personal religious convictions, Holman Hunt decided to visit the Holy Land to see and paint the Biblical locations for himself. His first visit lasted two years, 1854–56. During this time he traveled around Palestine and, as he did so, Biblical realism took over from the Pre-Raphaelite symbolic realism. He returned to England in 1856 and showed *The Scapegoat*, a painting of an old goat standing on the parched shore of the Dead Sea. The goat is a symbol of Christ carrying all the sins of the world on his shoulders, but is also the bearer of truth.

In total Holman Hunt made four journeys to the Holy Land, painting the landscape and religious scenes. His burning ambition was to find the actual locations where Biblical events happened, and then paint them. These paintings were generally well received and he became rich on the reproduction rights of his Palestine pictures.

Holman Hunt had a limited degree of success in his lifetime, he never became an influential artist as he so desperately wanted; and never had any followers despite having a long working life. In his lifetime he became best known as a religious painter and made a very comfortable living from his religious works, which still contained the Pre-Raphaelite's elaborate symbolism. For his early works he took a lot of unfair criticism, so much so that he seriously considered emigrating abroad, but he was tough and strong-minded enough to carry on working in the style he wanted. In 1852 he applied for associate membership of the R.A. but was turned down. Proud man that he was, he never applied again.

The Festival of St Swithin by William Holman Hunt showing the characteristic Pre-Raphaelite minute attention to detail and truth to nature. The painting started as an artistic exercise by Brown for his sister Emily, but when she gave up in despair he obliterated all her work and completed the painting himself.

ARTHUR HUGHES
1832–1915

A Londoner who studied at the R.A. Schools, Hughes became interested in the Pre-Raphaelites after reading *The Germ* in 1850. He made efforts to meet some of the members, successfully managing to encounter Hunt, Rossetti, and Brown that same year. In 1852 he exhibited *Ophelia*, a P.R.B. influenced painting and got to meet Millais, who was three years older than him. Hughes's own painting was very derivative but he possessed a real ability to absorb the essence of a painting style and reproduce it, which he successfully did for a time with the P.R.B.

Between about 1853–1870, Hughes did a string of very successful paintings in P.R.B. style and theme. However he wasn't invited to join their golden circle and he failed to live up to his first promise of *April Love*. He felt most affinity with Millais's style and, like him, became a painter of sentiment and love, specialising in scenes of meetings between lovers. His best known picture is *Home From the Sea*, which he painted outdoors in true P.R.B. fashion.

Through Rossetti he was briefly influenced by Blake and also by Arthurian subjects. In 1855 he started his best work and became a successful illustrator. He contributed to the Oxford Union decorations under Rossetti for a while, but he was essentially a sentimentalist not a visionary — he did not possess the natural talent and imagination to follow the second flowering of the P.R.B. He died at Kew in December 1915, seven years after his last painting was exhibited at the R.A.

JOHN WILLIAM INCHBOLD
1830–1888

Born in Leeds the son of a newspaper proprietor, as a young man Inchbold possessed a marked talent for precise and delicate drawings. He moved to London and became a pupil of the watercolorist Louis Haghe. He became perhaps the best, albeit briefly, of the P.R.B. strictly landscape painters, with a particularly evocative feeling for the freshness of spring in the countryside. To extend his range Inchbold went to Switzerland with John Ruskin in 1856 and 1858. But Ruskin bullied him ruthlessly over his drawings and paintings and was to blame when Inchbold lost confidence in his own style. Inchbold is most noted for *Ben Eay, Ross-shire*. In later years he traveled widely and then settled down in Switzerland between 1877–87. He published a volume of sonnets called *Annus Amoris* in 1876 and he died in Leeds in 1888.

FORD MADOX BROWN
1821–1893

Always an outsider to the art establishment who viewed him as suspiciously foreign because of his birth outside Britain, although to British parents, Ford Madox Brown studied art in the great schools of Antwerp and Paris and brought their influence to bear in his paintings. His pictures are now much in demand, but his contemporaries largely ignored his work and he never made much money out of painting. After visiting Rome in 1845 he became very influenced by the Nazarene School of painting, as

LEFT: *Cullin Ridge, Skye, from Sligachan* by John William Inchbold. He had a particular facility for landscapes and at one time was tutored and much encouraged by John Ruskin.

RIGHT: A detail of a girl holding a baby from the center foreground of *Work* by Ford Madox Brown. The dirty, ragged children are the lowest in society; the baby is a portrait of Arthur Gabriel Madox Brown.

ABOVE: A portrait of Ford Madox Brown by Millais.

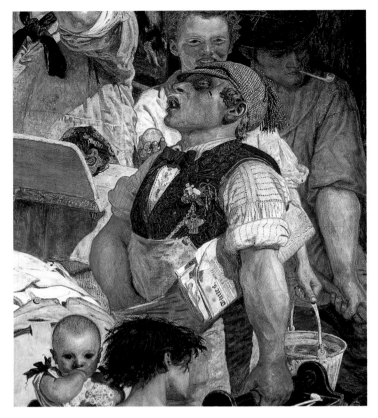

invented and practiced by the German painters Johann Overbeck (1789–1869) and Peter von Cornelius (1783–1875).

Madox Brown's work was highly original at a time when British art was mundane and predictable; his subjects were to do with English literature and language but produced in a dark, highly mannered, and dramatic style synthesized from his early European training and his tours of Italy and Switzerland. His work bore the brunt of his two great weaknesses — finishing and retouching. Even more so than Rossetti, he was almost incapable of finishing his paintings, this meant that he was never able to leave a work alone, even when it was ostensibly finished, he would continually retouch it, even though sometimes the painting was already sold.

Ford Madox Brown first met Dante Gabriel Rossetti in March 1848 and for a short time gave him academic painting lessons. This rather fell on deaf ears and Rossetti moved on, but in time they resumed their friendship. Ford Madox Brown became closely involved with the Pre-Raphaelite Brotherhood through his friendship with Rossetti, but never a member because he was regarded with xenophobic suspicion by Hunt and Millais.

Ironically it is Ford Madox Brown who in years to come became regarded as the ultimate Pre-Raphaelite because he painted many of their characteristic paintings. One such, the very first shown in the 1852 summer exhibition — The Pretty Baa-Lambs is a very Pre-Raphaelite-looking picture with its brilliant color (painted on a white ground), naturalistic detail and contemporary subject matter. He had often painted

TOP: Another detail from Work. This is the pot-boy from the nearby inn "The Princess of Wales." He is carrying a copy of The Times under his arm as he calls out his wares. He has apple blossom and a sprig of fuchsia in his button-hole above an elaborate fob, and carries two long-stemmed clay pipes on his tray.

ABOVE: Real workmen posed for Work to portray the noble navvies whose honest toil is the backbone of society. The principal workman is holding a pelargonium flower head between his lips.

Another detail from *Work*. The lady with the parasol is Brown's wife, Emma. In front of her is a ragged beggar woman holding a fistful of groundsel and clasping a basket of forget-me-nots and ferns.

out of doors before but this was the first time he had painted in natural light and it showed to anyone who looked properly. Unfortunately few did, the painting was hung in a poor position and went largely unnoticed.

The same year he enjoyed perhaps his best period and produced three of his finest paintings, all of them Pre-Raphaelite in everything except name: *The Last of England*, *An English Autumn* and *Work*. The latter, landmark, painting took him 13 years to finish. It is a modern allegory of society and a literal rendition of Heath Street, Hampstead. In it he shows ordinary people as heroes, but without a shade of sentimentality: at the center are common navvies digging. They are surrounded by a thronging crowd of contemporary people: ragged working class children and beggars alongside street traders and smart upper class ladies. The muscle workers are the navvies and itinerant farm workers, while the brain workers are two of Brown's heroes — the Reverend F.D. Maurice, a pioneer of working class education and Christian socialist, and Thomas Carlyle, the author of *Past and Present*.

Ford Madox Brown eventually made enough money from his paintings to buy a house in Fitzroy Square which became a lively center for artists and writers to gather together and swap ideas and gossip.

After receiving little notice for his work Brown gave up exhibiting at the R.A. after 1853; and by 1856 he had lost his belief in the Pre-Raphaelite ethos of painting modern morality works, instead he started collaborating with Morris and Co., working on designs for art glass and illustrations. He was commissioned to paint 12 large murals inside Manchester Town Hall showing the glorious history of Manchester, and he spent a great deal of time on the project, after which he played no significant part in artistic development.

JOHN EVERETT MILLAIS
1829–1896

Born into an affluent middle class family in Southampton, Millais was a naturally talented artist with an engaging, unspoiled personality. He became the youngest pupil ever at the R.A. Schools when he arrived there aged 11, and the youngest to complete the course five years later. Technically he was extremely competent and was the star pupil, but he was criticized for lacking a certain breadth of imagination and vision, which is ironic given his future as a Pre-Raphaelite.

For the Summer Exhibition of the R.A. in 1849 he painted *Isabella*, a story of passion, jealousy and murder from a poem by Keats after a story by Boccaccio. Millais depicted all these elements in Italianate style with intricate symbolic metaphors worked through both colors and objects: the passion flower hints at Isabella's true nature, while the blood orange she holds shows her passion will end in spilt blood, and a hawk ripping a white feather to pieces indicates the cruel nature of her two brothers, who go on to murder her lover. The work was generally well received, particularly for its early Renaissance quality of composition, colorings and slightly flat perspective.

The following year Millais painted himself into the furore that surrounded his picture *Christ in the Carpenter's Shop*. He lost a lot of the kudos he had gained previously as the Academy's most gifted pupil and aroused public doubts about his personal religious leanings. His other paintings of the time took themes from William Shakespeare; in *Ferdinand Lured by Ariel*; Millais tried his first major painting out of doors. Painted on a pure white ground the colors sing out in true Pre-Raphaelite fashion. The painting went to the R.A. in April 1850 where it was bought for £150.

The other Shakespearean painting, which excited him more in concept, was *Ophelia*, one of the greatest Pre-Raphaelite works of all. This shows Ophelia floating down the river into which she has cast herself, feeling, rejected by Hamlet. Her hair fans out in the stream, a necklace of violets around her neck and a loose bouquet of many different flowers drifting away from her slightly raised hands. All of these in Victorian flower lore contain meaning or are mentioned by Shakespeare in *Hamlet*. The plants on the riverbank show a typical selection of flowers and plants from an English summer hedgerow, all painted in precise detail. After casting around for a suitable location for the painting, he finally chose a quiet spot on the Hogsmill River (a tributary of the Thames) at Ewell in Surrey. Much of the walk was painted outdoors on the riverbank, greatly to the annoyance of a pair of swans who disputed the territory and drove Millais to near distraction. For convenience he took lodgings at Surbiton Hill, a few miles away, with his friend Holman Hunt.

For the 1851 R.A. Exhibition Millais produced three paintings, one of which, *The Woodsman's Daughter*, proved a great success and laid the foundations for his election to become an Associate of the Academy in November 1853 at age 24 — the earliest possible age. Only Sir Thomas Lawrence was elected younger. He then exhibited *The Huguenot*, a work showing a Catholic girl and her Huguenot lover on the day of the St. Bartholomew's Day Massacre in Paris, at the R.A. Exhibition in 1852. Interestingly this religiously-themed picture was conceived at the same time at Worcester Park Farm that Holman Hunt was developing ideas for *The Light of the World*. It was clearly an anti-Catholic picture painted at a time when religious paranoia over the intentions of the Pope were rife in England. The painting further cleared any popish doubts lingering over his earlier work *The Carpenter's Shop*.

In 1853 Millais was invited to join the Ruskins on holiday in Scotland, with the intention of painting two portraits, one of John Ruskin and another of his wife Effie, who had previously posed for him for *The Order of Release*. Millais stayed with them in the Trossacks for almost four months, in the course of which he painted the definitive picture of John Ruskin: he set him standing by a small but fast running stream with a background of interesting geological rocks and plants. The work took a long time as it was so meticulously painted, with pedantic attention to even the smallest details of Nature — in keeping, of course, with Ruskin's ideals. Soberly dressed in black, Ruskin holds his hat by his side and stares with a pensive but pleasant expression on his face. Had he any idea that at the same time the young artist was falling in love with his wife, and furthermore the feelings were reciprocated, Ruskin might well have canceled the project. In due course the Ruskins were to divorce.

In the mid-1850s Millais's style began to change, he continued with the Pre-Raphaelite attention to detail but changed his theme to ill-fated lovers, which suited his public and also his private state of mind until he was able to claim Effie as his own: this he

was able to do on July 3, 1855 after her scandalous divorce from Ruskin.

That same year Millais decided to embark on a painting that was beautiful in its own right without any attempt to tell a story. His models were four young girls, all under 13 years of age, chosen for their youth and beauty. They were to be shown standing around a pile of gently smoldering autumn leaves which they had just collected from their garden. The painting, which became known as *Autumn Leaves*, was designed to evoke a mood and a feeling of the transience of life and beauty — all is doomed to eventual decay, even the greatest innocence and beauty is overwhelmed by the passage of time. The painting is considered to be Millais's masterpiece. He wanted the picture to awaken the deepest religious reflections with its solemn air and restrained coloring. The work was influenced personally by Alfred Lord Tennyson, one of whose works he was illustrating at the time, in particular by his poem *The Princess*. Autumn and dead leaves are favorite images of the poet.

The painting was sold, sight unseen, for £700 before the R.A. Exhibition opened, to a collector from Bolton. He didn't like it and swapped it soon after with a Liverpool collector for three unremarkable paintings. The general feeling about the painting was that it was nice enough but what was it all about? Millais was anticipating the Impressionists and the public was not ready and the response was generally disappointing. So, he returned to his more accessible (and saleable) narratives of lovers, and as a result by 1856 Millais was the most successful painter in England. In testimony to this, the Academy Exhibitions of the mid to late 1850s are full of imitations of his work. In the 1860s Millais broadened out his style until it lost all resemblance to the work of the early Pre-Raphaelites.

Having started out as a young firebrand, Millais became a stalwart establishment figure — even becoming a baronet — always faithful to the dictates of the R.A. He regularly showed at Academy exhibitions and became so influential there that he was made President in 1896, the same year that he died. His most talented follower was Arthur Hughes.

WILLIAM MORRIS
1834–1896.

William Morris personally affected more people's lives directly with his original ideas about design and home decoration than any of his Pre-Raphaelite predecessors or contempories. Through this he had enormous impact on the decorative arts and was an important influence on the Art Nouveau movement, which arose primarily in France around the turn of the century. Morris was not a natural painter, although he

A rare photograph of William Morris without his beard.

A woodblock of William Morris, one of the principals of the second wave of Pre-Raphaelites and the founder of the Arts and Crafts Movement.

Out of these co-operative endeavors the idea to establish a firm to make such furniture and furnishings for a wider public grew. Thus, in 1861, under the aegis of William Morris, a small firm called Morris, Marshall, Faulkner & Co. was created with the intention of bringing high quality craftsmanship into the lives of ordinary people. The firm was to design furniture, tapestries, wallpaper, tiles, art glass, carpets, and fabrics as well as jewelery and metalwork. They had impressive premises in Red Lion Square where the showrooms presented their work in specially designed sets giving the complete idealized medieval arts and crafts look they sought. A large number of friends and acquaintances arrived to work at the firm, each bringing their own specialities and abilities.

Morris was a workaholic who drove himself around the clock, getting in the commissions, designing, and helping to ensure that the products were made to the highest possible specification and then delivered on time to the customer. The first of these for the firm of Morris, Marshall, Faulkner & Co. were largely people with progressive taste who delighted in the return to craftsmanship values — most of them tended to be Gothic revival architects.

In 1862 Morris started designing wallpaper patterns, arguably the one thing for which he is best remembered and venerated. The first of many patterns were released to the public in 1864, the designs included "Trellis," "Fruit" and "Daisy" — patterns which are still very popular today. In tune with all decorative things medieval, Morris soon wanted to make huge and impressive tapestries. In 1877 he started weaving: he generally did the backgrounds and Burne-Jones the figures.

Morris hated the way the post-Industrial Revolution society was heading, destroying much of the countryside and old buildings to make way for a new and ugly mechanized society. He felt so strongly about this that in 1877 he founded the Society for the Protection of Ancient Buildings with the intention of not only preserving old buildings but guarding against poor restoration as well.

In 1890 William Morris founded the Kelmscott Press, his own private press, with the intention of raising the quality and standards of book production, design and printing. By then he was an important figure in the socialist movement, supporting an anti-industrial society and a return to quality hand-crafted production.

DANTE GABRIEL ROSSETTI
1828–82

The young Rossetti was encouraged by his cosmopolitan parents to use his vivid imagination to develop his passionate interests of drawing and

tried in his youth when encouraged by Rossetti, but rather he was a great designer.

Already a confident, gregarious, and rich young man — he had a private income of £900 a year, a very comfortable sum in those days — his life changed forever when he met Dante Gabriel Rossetti in 1856. Rossetti encouraged him to take up art as a livelihood and a lifestyle. Another turning point came when, much to his upper middle class parents' dismay, he married Jane Burden in 1859. Their misgivings centred around the fact that she was the daughter of an ostler and of dubious personal repute. Sadly their marriage did not prove to be a success. For their home Morris had the vision of a Palace of Art where Jane could be the centre and inspiration. He commissioned Philip Webb, an architect from his old practice, to design the Red House at Bexley Heath in Kent. All the furniture and furnishings were to be made by William Morris with the help of his friends. Morris became a great socialist after these collective efforts and devoted much of his time to developing socialist ideas.

A pencil sketch by Dante Gabriel Rossetti entitled *Mrs. Rossetti Reading*, dated April 30, 1870.

writing. All his life Rossetti was torn between his twin loves of poetry and painting — to such an extent that he regarded the two disciplines as inseparable. Arguably, with his facility and interest in both disciplines, he did himself a disservice as he never dedicated himself to either pursuit sufficiently to become a true master. In his youth he spent hours in the British Museum Reading Room soaking up as much literature as he could, to the detriment of his painting. Because of this he never developed the facility and ability of technique that would have helped him to become one of the really great painters; however he did become widely-read in German, French, and Italian.

Rossetti took the inspiration for his drawings from stories by his favorite authors, notably Shakespeare, Coleridge, Poe, Goethe, and, in particular, his chief obsession, Dante, with whom he felt a close affinity. Indeed he frequently annotated his paintings — usually on the frame — with poems and texts to explain and develop the pictorial narrative and often in particular explaining the elaborate symbolism. For example, for his first real P.R.B. painting *The Girlhood of Mary Virgin*, which he painted in Holman Hunt's

studio (at the same time as Hunt was painting *Rienzi*), he wrote two explanatory sonnets on the frame describing the meaning of the dove, the lamp, the rose, and the vine and his use of the symbolism of color: gold for charity, blue for faith, green for hope, and white for temperance.

Despite his lessons at the R.A., Rossetti never really got to grips with oil painting, and, discouraged by the academic teaching, he dropped out of the school and went instead to study under Ford Madox Brown who had distinct European leanings in his work. Rossetti had been swept away by his colorful, but naturalistic interpretations of stories, and his medieval-like pictures from stories by some of the great authors of English literature, all done in a Nazarene style. Rossetti met Brown after writing him such a flattering letter that the latter thought that he was just making fun of him and went round to remonstrate with the young man armed with a big stick. However, an initially distressed Rossetti managed to convince the skeptical Brown that he was indeed sincere in his praise and then, deeply flattered, Brown agreed to give him free painting lessons. These consisted of academic studies of bottles, jars, and phials of paint. Rossetti, restless as ever, was quickly bored and after a few months turned to his new friends, Holman Hunt and Millais, for advice and encouragement.

In common with the other Pre-Raphaelites, Rossetti met some critical hostility — although none of the vilification fired at his friends — for his early paintings. By 1850 he decided to try a work altogether more ambitious and much bigger physically. The first subject he chose was inspired by his contemporary, the poet Browning, but nothing came of it; he tried again with a picture of Dante and Beatrice, but he also abandoned this effort and had nothing to show at the R.A. exhibition of 1851. All this was symptomatic of a greater problem and after 1850 he gave up exhibiting in public; he had always been the least productive of the triumvirate, partly due to his lack of skill with oil paints but rather more to do with his chronic inability to actually get around to finishing a painting before getting distracted by another subject.

He worked painfully slowly, taking enormous amounts of time to get just the tiniest detail true to life. Ruskin, recognising his failings, tried encouraging him actually to finish a painting, but to little avail. Instead he turned much of his time and attention to writing poems and producing drawings — his favourite medium — and watercolors largely inspired by his readings. All the while he was progressing further and further away from Pre-Raphaelite modernism until he gave up contemporary subjects altogether and concentrated instead on old stories and legends. He also developed his own unique approach to using watercolors which, in essence, involved applying intricate layers of hatched and stippled color with a dryish brush, to produce a finished work that was not unlike art glass in effect.

Rossetti's themes often revolved around women, who, he believed, held the mystery of existence within themselves. He saw them as magical beings, shrouded in secrets and sensuality and he frequently explored the themes of female virtue, beauty, and passion until he excluded all other subjects completely. Such women he set into stories mainly from Dante, the Bible, and in particular, Morte d'Arthur.

Around 1853 Rossetti met and fell in love with Elizabeth Siddal, and for a period she obsessed him. Her face recurs again and again in his work, particularly in his richly detailed watercolors. They became engaged but Rossetti, ever the romantic, fell in love again, this time in Oxford in 1857, with the stunningly beautiful Jane Burden, then only 17 years old. She modelled for La Pia de' Tolomei and Rossetti, despite his best endeavors, found himself helplessly drawn to her. She did not return his feelings and married William Morris instead. Rossetti loved her from a distance for the rest of his life and painted her likeness again and again in his later years. Jane, more even than Lizzie, became the archetypal Pre-Raphaelite beauty, with her strong sensual face and masses of long flowing hair. They remained good and close friends long after her love for William Morris evaporated (and his for her).

After trying his hand at illustration using woodcuts — to varying degrees of success — Rossetti turned again to exploring Arthurian subjects. He made a scant living out of selling small, jewel-like watercolors to a select group of collectors, among whom Ruskin was one of the most important. He also painted a series of watercolors which were bought by William Morris as he finished them. Still these Arthurian/medieval courtly romance subjects galvanized him most and these culminated in a commission to decorate the Oxford Union Building in 1857. Needing someone to pose for Mary Magdelene, he hunted around trying a number of models, the most significant of which was Fanny Carnforth, a vivacious Londoner, who became in succession (probably) his model, mistress, and housekeeper. The work entailed in the Union Building was too much for a single artist to complete alone, so Rossetti recruited a group of young friends to help. They did not give themselves a name, but history has dubbed them the second wave of Pre-Raphaelites.

Now working in Oxford, his love for Lizzie faded but he still married her in 1860 although she was known to be dying. Neither of them had much money and he neglected her, preferring instead to dally with other women. Her health deteriorated and she died tragically young, two years later, by her own hand with laudanum, although the official verdict was accidental death. Deeply saddened but perhaps secretly relieved, Rossetti got on with his own life, first moving from their marital home, which contained too many memories, to Cheyne Walk in Chelsea. He appears to come to terms with his feelings for Lizzie in 1864–70 while he painted Beata Beatrix, ostensibly about Dante and Beatrix, but really about Lizzie. True to form, the painting is full of symbolism: the red dove is an emblem of death, while the sundial is pointing at the hour of nine, the time of her death; the poppy in her hands is the clearest indication of all, bringing as it does the sleep of death, in her case the opiate laudanum.

With the move to Chelsea, Rossetti changed other aspects of his life. He stopped writing poetry — he had thrown the manuscripts of his poems into Lizzie's grave — and gave up painting Arthurian subjects. Most importantly, he stopped seeing John Ruskin who had done so much to support him, especially in the difficult early years. The human company he kept was no longer excitingly bohemian but outright disreputable.

He also developed a strange fascination for animals which he started collecting in alarming numbers: wombats were a particular favorite, but he also had owls, woodchucks, parrots, peacocks, dormice, rabbits, kangaroos, wallabies, even a racoon, salamanders, lizards, a jackass and, last but not least, a Brahmin bull.

By this time Rossetti had given up all pretence of painting modern morality subjects and instead devoted himself to painting images of women in all their beauty. The compositions he put them in invariably conveyed his own personal state of mind and emotions. In the early days of his infatuation with Lizzie, his pictures of women conveyed innocence and virginal simplicity; in time these became much richer and more sensual as their relationship became physical. Later still, as his love for her faded, the paintings convey disenchantment and disappointment, of lost promises, wishing and hoping for the unattainable. The passage of time becomes a progressively important theme: everything is measured in time and man's slow passage through life to inevitable death.

Inevitably Rossetti lost his good looks, becoming fat and balding. He drank altogether too much and indulged in drugs. His overriding fear became that he would lose his sight, as his father had before him; this reckless abuse of his body left him sleepless and morbid, and his doctors diagnosed strain and nervous tension. To prevent insomnia he drank whisky before taking 10 grains of chloral; by the time he died he boasted he was taking 180 grains a day.

A photograph of the Rossetti family taken in their garden by the Rev. C. L. Dodgson — better known as Lewis Carroll, the author of *Alice in Wonderland*. From left to right: Gabriel, Christina, Frances and William.

A public attack on him in 1871 in an infamous pamphlet entitled *The Fleshy School of Poetry* confirmed his hitherto paranoid view that everyone was out to do him down. The following year he was so deeply depressed that he tried suicide, with laudanum. The attempt failed but his health never recovered. He went from bad to worse until he was partially paralysed by the lethal cocktail of morphia, laudanum, and chloral he kept taking, plus the whisky, claret, and brandy he drank to excess. He became a virtual recluse but throughout this time he still communicated by letter to a few select friends — none of whom realized the desperate state of his health — most notably Ford Madox Brown and Jane Morris, until he died 10 years later.

JOHN RUSKIN
1819–1900.

A very complex and deep-thinking man from an affluent, well-traveled background, Ruskin was a great watercolorist in his own right and a very meticulous draftsman who had a fine eye for detail and line. He had widespread interests including art, art history, architecture, mineralogy, agriculture, politics, and social reform. However, he made his fame and reputation as an art critic and thinker. He saw art as the medium through which morality and the truth of Nature should be expressed. Many of these thoughts he explored at length in his five volume magnum opus, *Modern Painters*. The second volume, about the relevance of Nature and naturalism and the need to return to late

LEFT: Recognizable from the Millais portrait, this is John Ruskin by Sir John Edgar Boehm, R.A. in 1880.

RIGHT: Frederick Sandys was a formidably good draughtsman as seen here with his interpretation of *Nepenthe* — a drug used by the ancients to obliterate their sorrows and alluded to in the poppies.

medieval and early Renaissance artistic values, proved pivotal in firing the imagination and enthusiasm of the young Pre-Raphaelites.

By defending the young artists Ruskin helped to give them a credibility that the art establishment was unwilling to consider, and that the public — before his explanations of their elaborate thinking and symbolism — completely misunderstood. However, by bringing them to some artistic acclaim and an element of respectability, he expected in return to direct their artistic endeavors in line with his own theories and ideas. In this he was disappointed.

In particular, Ruskin took to the young Millais whom he considered to have the greatest talent; in consideration of this Ruskin invited him to join him and his wife on holiday in Scotland, with the intention of doing a portrait of each of them. This Millais did but he also fell in love with Ruskin's wife, who returned his feelings. The Ruskins eventually divorced in 1854 after seven turbulent years of marriage, and the lovers married. Inevitably Ruskin and Millais became estranged and Ruskin turned his attention to Rossetti, whose visionary ideas appealed to him. However, he was again frustrated with the artist, this time because of his chronic slowness and seeming inability to finish a canvas.

In his later years Ruskin became increasingly bitter at the industrialization of the country he loved and raged at the increasing mechanization all around him and its alienation to all things natural. He particularly hated the excesses of Victorian Gothic architecture which, ironically, he was in part responsible for reviving. He moved out of London, initially to Oxford as Slade Professor of Art, and then on to the Lake District where he made his home at Brantwood on the edge of Coniston Water. Once there, he gave up his interest in architecture and concentrated instead on trying to re-create a peasant society through cottage life and industry. After 1869 he lost his senses and became certifiably mad.

ANTHONY FREDERICK AUGUSTUS SANDYS
1829–1904
Sandys was born in Norwich, the son of a professional painter and one-time drawing master. Although a largely self-taught artist, he made a modest living by selling his architectural and antiquarian drawings to his patron — the Rev. James Bulwer, the Rector of Stody. Sandys was a precociously good draftsman, and he won the Royal Society of Arts medals in 1846 and 1847. In 1851 Sandys came to London where he exhibited at the R.A. for the first time. He mainly specialized in illustration and portrait drawing, but decided to extend his range by trying oils in late

1850s. At much the same time, around 1857, he became a friend of Rossetti with whom he stayed at 16 Cheyne Walk for most of 1866. In October they went on a walking tour but fell out soon after. In the 1860s Sandys made woodcuts for the magazine *Once a Week*. He became a founder member of the International Society of Sculptors, Painters and Gravers in 1898. He died 1904 in London.

THOMAS SEDDON
1821–1856
Born in the City of London, Seddon was the son of a cabinet-maker at which trade he became apprenticed at age 16. He soon developed an ambition to become a painter, and while still cabinet-making, took painting and drawing classes. There he developed a meticulous technique and became a painstaking draftsman. In 1849 he visited North Wales and for the first time really tried his hand at landscapes. He continued on when he went to Barbizon in France in 1850. Around this time he became a friend of Rossetti and, through him, became familiar with the work of the P.R.B. That same year he suffered a severe attack of rheumatic fever, with recovery from near-death he turned to Christianity, vowing to visit the Holy Land.

Seddon painted landscapes in the true P.R.B. manner, although Ruskin called him a "prosaic Pre-Raphaelite" due to the ruthlessness and lack of sentimentality with which he rendered his landscapes. When camping with Holman Hunt in the desert while on their way to the Holy Land in 1854 he painted *The Great Sphinx at the Pyramids of Gizeh*. He stayed abroad for over a year. A religious man, he was deeply moved to be in the Holy Land and felt it his mission to present an accurate record of the landscape. He got back to London in 1855 after a brief stay in France. His best known painting is *The Valley of Jehoshapat*, which is almost photographic in its detail and observation; it was unsold in his lifetime. He returned to Egypt in autumn 1856 but died of dysentery in Cairo in November. His friends drew up a subscription to buy *The Valley of Jehoshapat,* which they presented to the National Gallery. Never a prolific artist, he left very few works.

RIGHT: Portrait of *Elizabeth Siddal Playing a Stringed Instrument* by Rossetti. They married in 1860, but they were not destined to be happy together.

LEFT: A pen and ink portrait of the young Elizabeth Siddal dated February 6, 1855. She became a successful painter herself but has been overshadowed by the male artists around her.

RIGHT: The only sculptor in the group, Thomas Woolner found work hard to come by in his youth and only in later years did he manage to establish himself as a successful artist making portrait busts. This is of Thomas Combie.

ELIZABETH SIDDAL
1829–1862

One of the great Pre-Raphaelite muses — especially for Dante Gabriel Rossetti — she was a remarkably striking beauty with glowing copper hair and dramatic green eyes. She was first noticed working in a West End milliner's shop and posed for Holman Hunt's *Valentine Rescuing Sylvia from Proteus*, but she soon worked exclusively for the jealously possessive Rossetti who fell in love with her in 1851. She became Rossetti's mistress and then wife in 1860. Under his influence she became a painter herself and was much encouraged in turn by John Ruskin. Her health started to fail her, and, coupled with the loss of Rossetti's love, she took too many opiates. These took their due toll and killed her in 1862.

JAMES ABBOTT McNEILL WHISTLER
1834–1903.

A contemporary of the Pre-Raphaelites, although American he spent much of his life in England and in Europe. He enjoyed his student days in Paris with, among others, Gustave Corbet. He was very taken with Japanese prints, which influenced his work in term of design and color. In the 1860s he settled in London and for a time was in close contact with the Pre-Raphaelites. Rossetti in particular influenced his use of figures and drapery. He exhibited the

Symphony in White at the Salon des Refusés in 1863. Stylistically he bridges the gap between the Pre-Raphaelites and the Impressionists.

THOMAS WOOLNER
1825–1892

From Hadleigh in Suffolk, Woolner's only real claim to fame is as one of the original founders of the P.R.B. At the time he was a moderately talented, 23-year-old sculptor and amateur poet. He went to train at the R.A. Schools in 1842. There he became a friend of Rossetti who nominated him for the P.R.B.; he then met Hunt and Millais and they all agreed that their views on truth to Nature applied equally to sculpture. They responded to his burning ambition to bring truthfulness and a strong poetic spirit to his work. However, he became increasingly bitter towards the Academy for its lack of enthusiasm and promotion for sculpture. Woolner introduced Coventry Patmore to the circle and became great personal friends with Tennyson.

Woolner left the P.R.B. in despair after smashing all his clay maquettes, enraged at his failure to obtain a commission to sculpt a Wordsworth memorial. In July 1852 he sailed to Australia to pan for gold, staying there for some years but without making his fortune. Inspired by the departure of Woolner to foreign climes, Ford Madox Brown painted *The Last of England* as a tribute to the courage and strength of the vast number of emigrants leaving British shores.

Soon Woolner was making a much better living from supplying colonists in Sydney and Melbourne with medallions and busts. Meanwhile, in 1853 back in London, his P.R.B. friends gathered together only once to do portraits of each other to send to Woolner.

In 1854 he returned to London, where he slowly established a successful practice in portrait busts. He became professor of Sculpture at the R.A. for 1877–9. After 1870 Woolner received major commissions for public monuments, Queen Victoria in Birmingham, Palmerston in London, Lawrence in Westminster Abbey and many more. He died in London in 1892.

The Seeds and Fruits of English Poetry 1845-51
Ford Madox Brown
Oil on canvas, 13⅜ x 18⅛in.
Ashmolean Museum, Oxford

Isabella c. 1849
John Everett Millais
Oil on canvas.
Guildhall Art Gallery,
Corporation of
London/Bridgeman Art
Library

45

**John Wycliffe Reading His Translation of the Bible to John
of Gaunt** 1847-48 1859-61
Ford Madox Brown
Oil on canvas, 47 x 60½in.
Bradford Art Galleries & Museums/Bridgeman Art Library

Ferdinand Lured by Ariel 1849-50
John Everett Millais
Oil on panel, 25½ x 20in.
Private Collection/Bridgeman Art Library

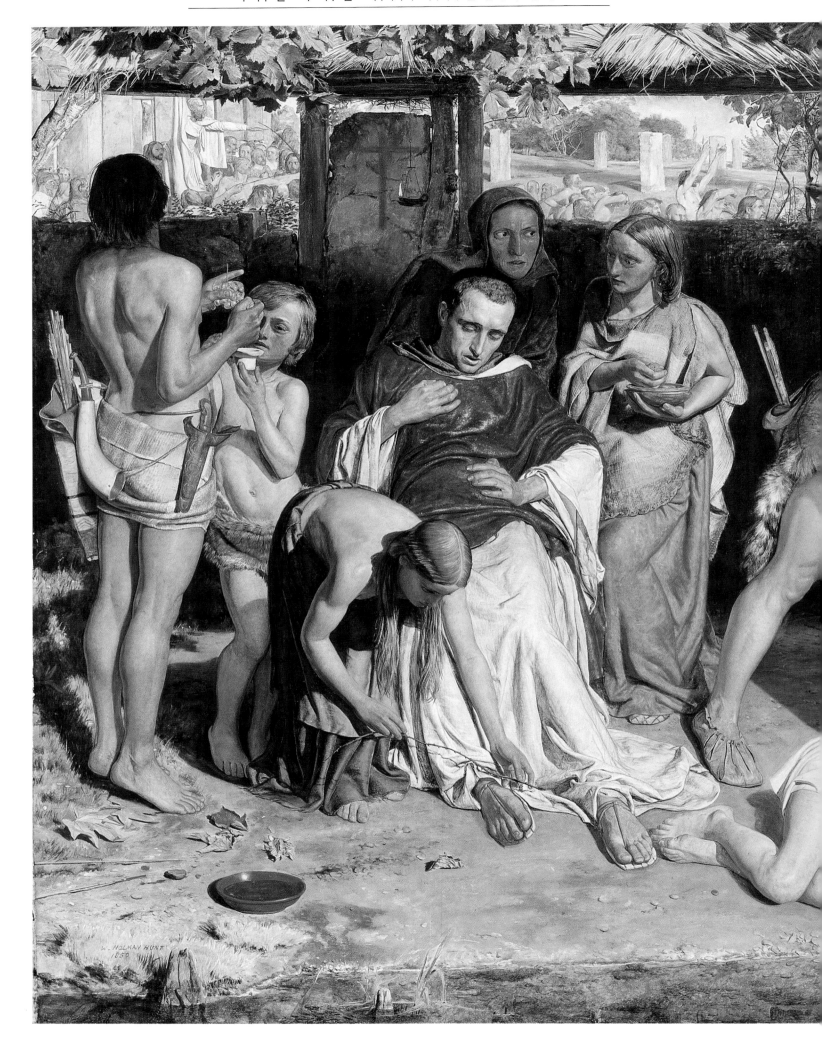

**Early Britons Sheltering a Missionary
from the Druids** 1849-50
William Holman Hunt
Oil on canvas, 43¾ x 52½in.
Ashmolean Museum, Oxford

Christ in the House of His Parents 1849-50
John Everett Millais
Oil on canvas, 34 x 55in.
Tate Gallery, London, 1997

51

Claudio and Isabella 1850-53
William Holman Hunt
Oil on panel, 30½ x 18in.
Tate Gallery, London, 1997

SICUT LILIUM

Convent Thoughts 1850-51
Charles Allston Collins
Oil on canvas, 32½ x 22¾in.
Ashmolean Museum, Oxford

Ophelia 1851-2
John Everett
Millais
Oil on canvas,
30 x 44in.
Tate Gallery,
London, 1997

Ecce Ancilla Domini! (The Annunciation) 1849-50
Dante Gabriel Rossetti
Oil on canvas , 28⅛ x 16½in.
Tate Gallery, London, 1997

Mariana in the Moated Grange 1850-51
John Everett Millais
Oil on panel, 23½ x 19½in.
Makins Collection/Bridgeman Art Library

**The Hireling
Shepherd**
1851-52
William Holman Hunt
Oil on canvas,
30$\frac{1}{16}$ x 43$\frac{1}{8}$in.
Manchester City Art
Galleries/
Bridgeman Art Library

Return of the Dove to the Ark 1851
John Everett Millais
Oil on canvas, 34½ x 21½in.
Ashmolean Museum, Oxford

The Light of the World 1851-53
William Holman Hunt
Oil on canvas over panel, 49⅜ x 23½in.
Keble College, Oxford/Bridgeman Art Library

The Pretty Baa-Lambs c. 1851–9
Ford Madox Brown
Oil on panel, 7¾ x 10⅛in.
Ashmolean Museum, Oxford

The Eve of St Agnes 1863
John Everett Millais
Watercolour, 10⅝ x 12¼ in.
Ashmolean Museum, Oxford

**Our English Coasts, 1852
(Strayed Sheep)** 1852
William Holman Hunt
Oil on canvas, 17 x 23in.
Tate Gallery, London, 1997

The Last of England 1852-5
Ford Madox Brown
Oil on panel, 32½ x 29½in.
Birmingham City Museums & Art Gallery/Bridgeman Art Library

The Awakening Conscience 1853-4
William Holman Hunt
Oil on canvas, 30 x 22in.
Tate Gallery, London, 1997

A Pet Exhibited 1853
Walter Howell Deverell
Oil on canvas, 54¼ x 30½in.
Tate Gallery, London, 1997

Found 1853-82
Dante Gabriel Rossetti
Oil on canvas, 36 x 31½in.
Delaware Art Museum, Wilmington/Bridgeman Art Library

The Blind Girl 1854-6
John Everett Millais
Oil on canvas, 32½ x 24½in.
Birmingham City Museums & Art Gallery/Bridgeman Art Library

The Doubt: 'Can These Dry Bones Live?' 1854-5
Henry Alexander Bowler
Oil on canvas, 23½ x 19⁹⁄₁₆in.
Tate Gallery, London, 1997

The Great Sphinx at the Pyramid of Gizeh 1854
Thomas Seddon
Watercolour and bodycolour, 9¾ x 13¾in.
Ashmolean Museum, Oxford

Mother and Child 1854-6
Frederick George Stephens
Oil on canvas, 18½ x 25¼in.
Tate Gallery, London, 1997

In Early Spring 1855
John William Inchbold
Oil on canvas, 21 x 14in.
Ashmolean Museum, Oxford

April Love 1855
Arthur Hughes
Oil on canvas, 35 x 19½in.
Tate Gallery, London, 1997

Chatterton 1856
Henry Wallis
Oil on canvas, 24½ x 36¾ in.
Tate Gallery, London, 1997

The Wounded Cavalier 1856
William Shakespeare Burton
Oil on canvas, 35 x 41 in.
Guildhall Art Gallery, Corporation of London/Bridgeman Art Library

The Scapegoat 1854
William Holman Hunt
Oil on canvas, 33¾ x 54½in.
Lady Lever Art Gallery, Port Sunlight/Bridgeman Art Library

Work 1852, 1856-63
Ford Madox Brown
Oil on canvas,
53$^{15}/_{16}$ x 77$^{11}/_{16}$in.
Manchester City Art
Galleries/Bridgeman Art
Library

Autumn Leaves 1855-56
John Everett Millais
Oil on canvas, 41 x 29in.
Manchester City Art Galleries/Bridgeman Art Library

The Wedding of St. George and Princess Sabra 1857
Dante Gabriel Rossetti
Watercolour on paper, 14⅜ x 14⅜ in.
Tate Gallery, London, 1997

**Pegwell Bay, Kent — A
Recollection of October 5th
1858** 1858-60
William Dyce
Oil on canvas, 25 x 35 in.
Tate Gallery, London, 1997

Thoughts of the Past 1858-9
John Roddam Spencer Stanhope
Oil on canvas, 34 x 20in.
Tate Gallery, London, 1997

Gentle Spring c. 1860
(Anthony) Frederick Augustus Sandys
Oil on canvas.
Ashmolean Museum, Oxford

Dantis Amor 1860
Dante Gabriel Rossetti
Oil on mahogany, 29½ x 32in.
Tate Gallery, London, 1997

Sidonia von Bork 1860
Edward Burne-Jones
Watercolour and gouache on paper,
13 x 6¾in.
Tate Gallery, London, 1997

La Belle Iseult 1858
William Morris
Oil on canvas, 28⅛ x 20in.
Tate Gallery, London, 1997

The Woodman's Child 1860
Arthur Hughes
Oil on canvas, 24 x 25¼in.
Tate Gallery, London, 1997

The Last Day in the Old Home 1862
Robert Braithwaite Martineau
Oil on canvas, 42¼ x 57in.
Tate Gallery, London, 1997

The Railway Station 1862
William Powell Frith
Oil on canvas.
Royal Holloway & Bedford New College, Surrey/Bridgeman Art Library

Beata Beatrix c1864-70
Dante Gabriel Rossetti
Oil on canvas, 34 x 26in.
Tate Gallery, London, 1997

Elijah Restoring the Widow's Son c. 1864
Ford Madox Brown
37 x 24⅛ in
Victoria and Albert Museum/Bridgeman Art Library

Home From Sea 1863
Arthur Hughes
Oil on panel, 20 x 25⅜in.
Ashmolean Museum, Oxford

Monna Vanna 1866
Dante Gabriel Rossetti
Oil on canvas, 35 x 34in.
Tate Gallery, London, 1997

The Beloved 1865-6
Dante Gabriel Rossetti
Oil on canvas, 32½ x 30in.
Tate Gallery, London, 1997

The Sleeping Beauty
1860
Edward Burne-Jones
Oil on canvas.
Manchester City Art
Galleries/Bridgeman Art
Library

The Beguiling of Merlin 1870-74
Edward Burne-Jones
Oil on canvas, 73 x 43½in.
Lady Lever Art Gallery, Port Sunlight/Bridgeman Art Library

Astarte Syriaca 1877
Dante Gabriel Rossetti
Oil on canvas, 72 x 42in.
Manchester City Art Galleries/Bridgeman Art Library

Dreamers 1882
Albert Moore
Oil on canvas, 27 x 47in.
Birmingham City Museums & Art Gallery/Bridgeman Art Library

The Triumph of the Innocents 1883-4
William Holman Hunt
Oil on canvas, 61½ x 100in.
Tate Gallery, London, 1997

The Golden Stairs 1876-80
Edward Burne-Jones
Oil on canvas, 109 x 46in.
Tate Gallery, London, 1997

King Cophetua and the Beggar Maid 1884
Edward Burne-Jones
Oil on canvas, 109 x 46in.
Tate Gallery, London, 1997

Midsummer 1887
Albert Moore
Oil on canvas, 63 x 61in.
Russell-Cotes Art Gallery & Museum, Bourn/Bridgeman Art Library

The Lady of Shalott 1888
J. W. Waterhouse
Oil on canvas, 60½ x 78¾in.
Tate Gallery, London, 1997

The Bath of Psyche Exhibited 1890
Frederick Leighton
Oil on canvas, 74½ x 24½in.
Tate Gallery, London, 1997

Flora 1894
Evelyn de Morgan
Oil on canvas, 78 x 34in.
The de Morgan Foundation/Bridgeman Art Library

The Blessed Damozel 1895
John Byam Liston Shaw
Oil on canvas, 37 x 71in.
Guildhall Art Gallery, Corporation of London/Bridgeman Art Library

A Coign of Vantage 1895
Sir Lawrence Alma-Tadema
Oil on canvas, 25¼ x 17¾in.
Private Collection/Bridgeman Art Library

The Magic Circle 1886
J. W. Waterhouse
Oil on canvas, 72 x 50 in.
Tate Gallery, London, 1997

ACKNOWLEDGEMENTS

The Publisher is grateful to the following institutions for permission to reproduce the the pictures on the pages noted below:

Ashmolean Museum, Oxford: 24, 25, 26, 28 (top left), 33, 36, 37, 39, 40, 41, 42-3, 48-9, 53, 60, 62, 63, 72-3, 76, 91, 104-5.

Barnaby's Picture Library: 7, 9 (both), 10, 11 (both), 15 (both), 19 (bottom left), 20, 31, 32, 35.

Birmingham City Museums & Art Gallery: 66, 70, 112-3.

Bison Picture Library: 19 (top left and right).

Bradford Art Galleries & Museums: 46.

Bridgeman Art Library, London: Back cover, 1, 13, 22-3, 27, 28 (top and bottom right), 29, 44-5, 46, 47, 57, 58-9, 61, 63, 66, 69, 70, 80-1, 82-3, 84-5, 86, 100-1, 103, 108-9, 110, 111, 112-3, 118-9, 123, 124-5, 126.

Delaware Art Museum, Wilmington: 69.

Guildhall Art Gallery, Corporation of London: 44-5, 80-1, 124-5.

Harvard University Art Museums: 18.

Keble College, Oxford: 61.

Lady Lever Art Gallery, Port Sunlight: Back cover, 82-3, 110.

Makins Collection: 57.

Manchester City Art Galleries: 1, 13, 22-3, 27, 28 (top and bottom right), 29, 58-9, 84-5, 86, 108-9, 111.

Royal Holloway & Bedford College, Surrey: 100-1.

Russell-Cotes Art Gallery & Museum: 118-9.

Tate Gallery, London, 1997: Front cover, 2, 4, 17, 50-1, 52, 54-5, 56, 64-5, 67, 68, 71, 74-5, 77, 78-9, 87, 88-9, 90, 92-3, 94, 95, 96-7, 98-9, 102, 106, 107, 114-5, 116, 117, 120-1, 122, 127.

The de Morgan Foundation: 123.

Victoria and Albert Museum, London: 103.